Songs from the Few to the Many

Leon J. Gratton

Grosvenor House
Publishing Limited

All rights reserved
Copyright © Leon J. Gratton, 2018

The right of Leon J. Gratton to be identified as the author of this
work has been asserted in accordance with Section 78
of the Copyright, Designs and Patents Act 1988

The book cover picture is copyright to Inmagine Corp LLC

This book is published by
Grosvenor House Publishing Ltd
Link House
140 The Broadway, Tolworth, Surrey, KT6 7HT.
www.grosvenorhousepublishing.co.uk

This book is sold subject to the conditions that it shall not, by way of
trade or otherwise, be lent, resold, hired out or otherwise circulated
without the author's or publisher's prior consent in any form of binding or
cover other than that in which it is published and
without a similar condition including this condition being imposed
on the subsequent purchaser.

This book is a work of fiction. Any resemblance to
people or events, past or present, is purely coincidental.

A CIP record for this book
is available from the British Library

ISBN 978-1-78623-157-4

Hey Momma

Hey Momma gonna
Make you sing
Make you love
Everything

Hey darling gonna
Make you dance
Gonna love you
Every chance
Oh yeah
Oh yeah

Hey Momma gonna
Make you smile
And show you love
Like a child

There Momma we're stuck again
Dying of boredom in the rain
Oh yeah
Oh yeah

Hey Momma gonna make you cry
Gonna show you how I'm your guy

Hey Momma when everything's fine
That's when you know love's on time

Hey Momma gonna make you mine
Gonna show you that you really shine

Hey momma be brave
Cause it ain't the first time that I'm your slave
Oh yeah
Oh yeah

ATTITUDE

Born with an attitude
I wander at the wheel
Bug boy got the gratitude
While I burn the fuel

Storm in with attitude
Iron horses with a feel
Strange man the devil's statue
Satan's slaves with fuel

Born with no gratitude
To a world with the devil's wheel
Love is just an attitude
With girls that are unreal

Riders of the delude
With quiet men of steel
Gone is my gratitude
To a piece of the devil's fuel

My morning of attitude
Is wandering the field
Sons with the gratitude
Whilst I run with the steel

Na Na Na Na
Born with an attitude
Na Na Na Na
Born with an attitude
Na Na Na Na
Born with an attitude
Born with an attitude
Na Na Na Na

SKINNY BACK BABY

Skinny back baby
Remind me you are a lady
Baby come into my sights
Baby I've got you ain't that right

Skinny back baby
Show me my unknown payday
Baby Baby be my one
Baby baby love the kingdom's son

Skinny back baby
Juice me up in my head
Baby baby you've wrecked my bed
Baby baby tears fell from me like lead

Skinny back baby
Show me you're a lady
Baby baby come let me love you
Baby baby let me be your quiet man

Skinny back baby
Skinny back baby
Be my woman
Be my lady

Devil woman crossed my floor
Kissed me gently and closed my door
Skinny back baby
Don't leave me too sore

Made with heaven in your eyes
I hate to say this but it's just a disguise
Skinny back baby
I've seen through your lies

Secrets you keep whilst poison weeps
It's on knives and broken glass I sleep
Skinny back baby
My soul you keep

Skinny back baby
Be my lady
I'm yours to keep your baby
Skinny back baby
Skinny back baby
Skinny back lady

I GOT WHAT I GOT

I was once in love with you
You tore down the dark
And at once I was no longer blue
I can't put you down
As broken as thunder to sound

Well, wishing for you night and day
My broken body made from clay
Then angels sang
And demons ran
I suppose salvation is away

The night broke free and then someone said to me
Love what you've got
Take note then take your best shot
I got what I got
I got what I got
I got what I got
I got what I got

Well this is starry eyed times

And people seem to love the sublime

The monster of madness close to learn

The people of sadness shall awake from their fears

It's simple when you share

I got what I got

I got what I got

I got what I got

Freedom the myth in unknown skies

Take some of heaven and leave

The disturbed lies

Prince of the towers

Quiet in the mist

Oh please be my baby

As now I know I exist

I got what I got

I got what I got

I got what I got

The sullen sun sunk deep in the sky

I turn away and save a goodbye

Quietly afraid of nights in disguise

A treasure trove to play

I let tears fall from my eyes

The world with its future
The soldier the butcher
Shall turn in on himself
Wishing quietly for wisdom's health
I got what I got
I got what I got
I got what I got
I got what I got

DIAMOND TEARS

My baby don't know me
Don't know me at all
My baby don't know me
Don't know me at all

My baby don't know me
Even tho' I'm ten feet tall
My baby don't know me
And diamond tears come to call

My baby don't know me
Don't know me at all
My baby don't know me
Through poppy fields I call

HERE I COME

Well baby here I come you know
The shaded one
I got the poppy the pills
The sweet Jane
I've seen things that would drive
Most insane
I hear those heels walk by most every night
And if you ain't female
Don't do it in the light

L.S.D popping pills playing night
Games so I'll say it once
Before you drive away
You can do what you want
But you don't get paid

The claw on my key chain
Says I got every right
So girl let's move through the night
The shaded one with Morrison in his vein
Says it once then sees if you'll stay
Do what you want but you don't get paid

The class A's leaving through the door
I don't care if all you want to do is score
The lower down the softer we become
You know me the shaded one

So girl looking so fine don't you
Know this ain't no wine and dine

Its case straight from the start
You know now I gotta a broken Heart
So like I said right from the start

You can do what you want
But you don't get paid
Do what you want but you
Don't get paid
You can do what you want
But you don't get paid

STATE FUNDED MILLIONAIRE

Life is going a thousand ways at once
With politics war and an unknown front
Piercing scream that deafens every ear
We turn
We live
We change in fear

Great, she cries, I'm the one being charged
For a bastard son
I wish things could be different
But the game you played was a dangerous one
And a rule shouldn't change on the kingdom's son

State funded millionaire
He walks by no one cares
We want some
But psychotic trance
Has become in some

The price we pay for a quiet life
Whether it be with power or a tender wife
But some can't hear the heart beat

Of a narcotic street

We turn

We live

We change in fear

State funded millionaire

He walks by no one cares

We want some

But psychotic trance

Has become in some

Jesus I believe temptations a ride

But if she does it again I'll tan her hide

The sweet bliss of torn through mists

Reminds us we almost lost this world State funded millionaire

He walks by no one cares

We want some

But psychotic trance

Has become in some

The fair the stare

The state funded millionaire

The shades the blades

Show the state funded millionaire

SOUL SUGAR

Soul sugar wonder whether you'll come
Heart on fire you know I gotta run
Come on baby got to feel your drug
Soul sugar become my love
Your raven hair
Your starlight eyes
Soul sugar yeah
Soul sugar you are the one
Ooooh

Star maker set into my heart and love
Soul sugar oh baby please come
Earth shaker you really move me
Earth shaker come on groove baby
Your raven hair
Your starlight eyes
Soul sugar yeah
Soul sugar you are the one
Ooooh

Soul sugar set into my blood
Earth shaker love me and come

Soul sugar you are ooh the one
Your summer shower fresh in its ways
Soul sugar be my girl
Soul sugar be my world
Soul sugar with passion in those eyes
Soul sugar you would light up the night
Soul sugar oooh yeah
Soul sugar oooh yeah
Soul sugar you are the best

WINSOME

The closeness a pill
That little piece of heaven
With love it's only thrill

My heart on the line
Yes you look so fine
My words simple in this world
Yes I'm hoping you'll be my girl

The closeness a pill
With wonderment in this world
With love its thrill

You are a dream to behold
Where I set my love and soul
On my sleeve with me being an ex- thief
You should feel deeply and believe

The closeness a pill
Peel it away dust in the coffee
With love its only thrill

Take me for what I am
An addict to love and drugs
It's set to hard'nd wood
And mystical magical rugs

The closeness a pill
That heart on the scales the feather
With love it's only thrill

You wonder if I'm going to devils trust
But needles to me are just bones
And the stings that come don't make me a jagger
So please let me show you comfort, another home
The closeness a pill
The world comes to you
You will know I sent that thrill

POETIC INTERLUDE

The way I look will change in ways
And sombre prayers turn into sayings
Ancient in zeal the pills bitter
But it's warmer than being numb
And if it's for you peel
Turn this world markings on the wall
With a delight it may call
Every girl I love will come to call
Apologises accepted, winsome all

The closeness a pill
The world comes to you
With love it's only thrill
The world comes to you
You will know I sent those pills
You are the one
You are the one
Winsome
Winsome
Winsome

DRAG

Going across the border
With a book on philosophical disorder
The neurosis breaking into anxiety
Depression the blues on the order

It's a drag being a mojo man
It's a drag becoming this rag

Witness me build up this scene
Listening intently for a scream
The beats across the border
And things look different when you're a soldier

It's a drag being a mojo man
It's a drag becoming this rag

Saviour or slave we cross past the scheme
The breaking of a heart I can feel that pain
Slowly driven these children of the rain
The cold howling moon drives you insane

It's a drag being a mojo man
It's a drag becoming this rag

It's a drag running in this tomb
It's a drag
It's a drag
It's a drag
It's a drag

CHILDREN OF THE FLOWERS

The people wonder at a raw sound
I know why the world turns
I know stars are round
Light up my world
Light up my world girl

I have strength coming in the morning sun
The feeling of love healing my broken heart
I screamed in the dark
I screamed in the night
Howling of moons
Dropping of spoons

The people wonder at a raw sound
I know why the world turns
I know stars are round
Light up my world
Light up my world girl

Ooo babe my mind is numb
Ooo babe I've been left dumb

Crazy crazy world of ours
Shows the way to children of flowers
Please remember freedom sometimes runs
Cold ooo so bold lovers we've become

STAR GLARES

Chase your dreamlike beauty oooh ahhh
Come to your melting heart oooh ahhh
I love the way you stand there oooh ahhh
Because the way is love. oooh ahhh

It's beginning to show
Your childlike presence
Your radiant glow oooh ahhh oh

Space out your movement oooh ahhh
Watch you don't lose it oooh ahhh
Your eyes of fire oooh ahhh
Look at me with desire oooh ahhh

It's beginning to show
Your childlike presence
Your radiant glow oooh ahhh

Become less in fury oooh ahhh
More is your beauty oooh ahhh
You are truly a child oooh ahhh
Born under a shining star oooh ahhh

It's beginning to show

Your childlike presence

Your radiant glow oooh ahhh

POEM

The foxy girl behind the counter

Sometimes she looks

Sometimes needs a reminder

That I play fair with this subtle

Beauty of raven hair

She hands me my dreams

And I think how happy she seems

Tho' some days to busy. But when I

Hear her singing I love her raven hair

Now night comes and I weep

For little do I sleep, just wonder If she cares

But I know she does.

In a world of star glares

OH THAT GIRL

Trace back into time
With thoughts spilling in a quiet mind
My heart open and sore
With beauty that I adore
Maybe she'll be my quiet loving slave
Or maybe she'll need tamed

Oh that girl
Oh that girl
Oh that girl that turns my world

Sleeping silent day but comes
I overdose on beauty you are the one
It's a world of narcotic bliss
And your heart and wickedness
It's a stolen glance but I can't persist
Town of hills
Skulls on dark graves
Curse this place I'm on my way

Oh that girl
Oh that girl
Oh that girl that turns my world

Well going down to the valley
With my pockets full of pills
The lizard man came
And showed me a world of chills
His echoing in my brain
Shows the girl is truly insane

Oh that girl
Oh that girl
Oh that girl that turns my world

It's insane with a broken heart
I think I'll need to watch for the dark
The girl is cold deathly and numb
I told her I'd wait till kingdom come
Yes the scaly crossed seasons
Give purity give me a reason
With open hearts and sullen ways
I didn't want to be by earth's shallow grave

Oh that girl
Oh the girl

Oh that girl who turns my world

Oh that girl

Oh that girl

Oh that girl who turns my world

SINGING IN THE DARKNESS

I have some time for you
Give me a chance I'll be true
Singing in the darkness
Singing those good ole blues

My world turns on through
Whilst creatures bloom in the new moon
Yours kisses hold me quiet hold me true
And life blushes to eyes of blue
Sometimes tears come and I cry right through

I have some time for you
Give me a chance I'll be true
Singing in the darkness
Singing those good ole blues

The holy houses which shine the lights
With passionate scream and dark delight
The mind of the people watch on and on
And I came to the conclusion bye throne
And question whether night runs us to the bone

I have some time for you
Give me a chance I'll be true
Singing in the darkness
Singing those good ole blues

BLOOD ON THE THREE OF CLUBS

Blood on the three of clubs
Going to games the word of slobs
Blood on the flag
With time moving away from us
Blood and gold
What really you have no soul

Well turn it twist it
Do what you like
Bye to the wonder
By to the night

Well the weapons of the Motorcycle War
Don't be so shallow we're all sore
My going on with words quiet
Blood is gone and shallow
I can tell you've been playing
With your shadow

Well turn it twist it
Do what you like
Bye to the wonder
Bye to the night

My cards all fucked up
With blood and fights
Sorry but you dealt me deaths delight
Go away to the people you love
The cops call
Blood on the three of clubs

Well turn it twist it
Do what you like
Bye to wonder
Bye to the night
Blood on the three of clubs
Blood on the three of clubs
Taken to distance
Yeah blood on the three of clubs

BOX OF BLUES

The score from the man
With blues the plan
10s going to get high
Leave those girls to sigh

It's on the man
It's our plan
Crying more, more

Indian candy lasts for days
With coffee crush I peel
Hoping for a score
There is a girl that I adore

It's on the man
It's our plan
Crying more more

The sleep I get is better than love
My worship of women goes with blues
None have been as true
Those Indian candy blues

It's on the man
It's our plan
Crying more more

The box filled with blues
But I'd rather be with you
Opiates move in my head
Closer I get to the dance of the dead

Our world of vapour and blues
Who knows what is true
You go to the small towers
With opium hearts and poppies
The sun hurts your eyes after a night on the blues

Well Valium gouch sleeping softly on the couch
Well dragon chased your sublime face
We want something to escape this world
And who knows that's why it's our girl
The morphine in the system with Indian swirl
Going on drugs cannabis light

JOKER'S GHOST

Burning up with drugs again
Burning up waiting for the rain
Torque the fuel give me the speed
Do you know the devil can?
You see him feed

Well well baby who hurts the most
Well well lover can you see
The joker's ghost

Hang me any way you can
Hang me and see pandemonium land
Upside down with halo burning up
Well hell In light whilst I light one up

RAG MAN

Woolly rag man
Came up to me and said
Whats the big plan
I said I'll buy but it'll
Be a tenner a bag man

Woolly rag man
Smiled and said
That's a done deal
It's called sandman
That woolly rag man

Chasin' spoons in a
Suicidal rag man's score
The woolly rag man
Brings pleasure bin less than
A gram

JACK OF DIAMONDS

My mind at peace

With Jokers dealt up my sleeve

The ace of hearts

Close to the jack of diamonds

You had me girl

You loved my world

Acid pushing and twisting

In a swirl

It's cold and cruel we've been fed It's cold and cruel in the dealer's head

My mind at peace

With Jokers dealt up my sleeve

The ace of hearts

Close to the Jack of Diamonds

Well well a tight world

You are a babe in a twirl

My mind racing, go on deal the six

Well I twist and pick up sticks

I smell the sandlewoood and crash on down

My mind at peace
With Jokers dealt up my sleeve
The ace of hearts
Close to the Jack of diamonds

The deal is crooked in this school
I look at your body and turn and drool
The pack is stacked
The deck boxed
Yes you take to many you've been out foxed

My mind at peace
With Jokers dealt up my sleeve
The ace of hearts
Close to the jack of diamonds

LIZARDS KINGS REST

Tranquilized deaths
Opium breathing breath
It's the world to some
Blonde hair
Lizard eyes that stare
Do it lady be my one

Well well it's here banded together
With opiate gear
I crush those pills
Put them in my coffee
Every day I watch the world

Fearful guests
Lizard hiss at dreams rest
My girl beautiful
With blonde hair
Yes yes the beauty is there
Please the day and the Lord won

Well well it's here banded
Together

With opiate gear
I crush those pills
Put them in my coffee
Every day I watch the world

Valium opiate on the scene
Very confusing
Gone the scream
Oh oh cancerous child
Should be out there running wild

JUMP AND SHOUT

My words are true
You want someone with old blue
You should take your time
My words are to climb

Hey hey hey move on
Hey hey hey groove on
Wait wait wait soothe some

Your body needs love
Yes your heart needs love
My world will shake and shout
You my girl is what it's all about

Hey hey hey move on
Hey hey hey groove on
Way way way jump and shout

CUTS TO THE BONE

If I cried in heaven
Would you leave me there?
If I lied at eleven
Would you forgive me?
If I smiled at roses
Would you take me through the poses?

I got to leave you alone
Nights so dark it cuts me to the bone

If I washed all the sin from your eyes
Would you say it was a monstrous disguise?
If I smiled begged and pleaded
Would you show me I'm needed?
If I wandered to the desert
Would you show me your treasure?

I got to leave you alone
Nights so dark it cuts me to the bone

CRY

Some days I quietly cry
Some days I hold onto the sky
Some days I pray we never said
Goodbye

Then comes night and I feel my guiding star
And some nights I take
To heaven with my star

The world around is split in two
And the girl I love has come
And gone to soon
Why can't faith hold me in its arms
Why doesn't love find me
In its charms

Some days I quietly cry
Some days I hold quietly
Onto the sky
Some days I pray we never
Said goodbye

Then comes night and I feel my
Guiding star
Some nights it takes me
Only so far

INSANE SUN

Here comes the night
Heavenly and open
The bright midnight
The very witching hour
11 until 1

Then comes the day
Some say salvation
Is the only way
Hearts break and mend
The dawning hour drives you
Round the bend

Unfolding mirrors
With unknown givers
First takers then fakers
Feigning their concern

Detoxing habits that some
Love yet hate
Shows how society serves up it's
Youth on a plate

Between us all the suns to blame
Giving us such beauty that it
Drives us insane

So here comes the night
The jewelled stars and cold moon
With hazes of blue which

Come too soon
Waste the dawn
Watch the sea
Become nearer to earth
And let it be

Reds and hues
I write on a purple midnight
A shimmering dawn who curses
We are all open to new ways

So gimme my bone
My very living way
And I'll pump and moan
Until you know what I say

Between us all the suns to blame
Giving us such beauty
That it drives us Insane

Insane sun
You are the one
Insane sun
You are the one

ACID BLUES

Love in romance
Take that chance
Hold me in your arms

It's a pulling way
With us being love filled slaves
The true eyes of beauty
Don't hold our love in regret

Love in romance
Take that chance
Hold me in your arms

Dawn I'm looking your way
And finality has beautiful ways
You are truly caught in a summer shower
Dance with me in the shadows of the tower

Love in romance
Take that chance
Hold me in your arms

Gone to godlike ways
It's in poetic charms
My redemption in a lover's soul
The acid blues show us unknown

Love in romance
Take that chance
Hold me in your arms
Show me lover's charms
The very light that you have shown
Whilst this feeling comes home
Love in romance
Take that chance
Hold me in your arms
Help me through this storm
Oh Dawn
Oh Dawn

POETIC INTERLUDE

Dawn of day in the unknown ways
Will become resolute in the winter's rays
With time we shall steal warm singing sayings
And with this become holy ones whilst
They think on love filled plays
The life you led was in the head
Of a man and poppy slaves
You turn your back and say okay
But loving is the only way

BLOOD DARK ON A DEVIL'S MOON

The novelty over and ships come in
The treasure trove gone no drugs
Well my heart bleeds red and gone
It's silent in this world with no
Friends only backstabbing cut throat
Guitars that lie

Help those souls
Help those souls
No harmony no control

The seeds of the temptress
Are more poison than Satan's soul
Price of nothing tell the same lie
And the more I close my fist
The tighter the tie
Been fed next to a junkies head

Help those souls
Help those souls
No harmony No control

With a night glowing
And someone sighing
I hear you sing
But this time it's out of tune

Blood dark on a devils moon
Blood dark on a devils moon
Blood dark on a devils moon

ARROW OF LOVE

Parma Violets is what I smell
All gone onto a day
Well well you sleep so nice
You just might take, take too much advice
Well the blues a baby the dues
I'll pay

It's worthwhile with me being
Cupid's son
Psyche tried to disown me
But Delphi won

Do it baby break my heart
The dozens that have
Well it's just roses in a park
My world in a spin with Valium
The quiet way you talk
Broken in by Jive on walk

It's worthwhile with me being
Cupid's son

Psyche tried to disown me
But Delphi won

Now lady you move with grace
Shallow but wonderful you
Paint your face
I see the liquor the drugs
The sun in heaven the earth rugs
Well I watch on with beauty in mind

It's worthwhile with me being
Cupid's son
Psyche tried to disown me
But Delphi won

Lizard eyes set to dreams
Nights of passion lustful screams
The warm summer night in gods land
I take my world to Juno's right red hand
So take what you've got please be careful
Because If you rest in peace
I'll cook up a shot

Well it's worthwhile with me being Cupid's son
Psyche tried to disown me
But Delphi won
Delphi won

Delphi won
Cupid's son
Cupid's son
The arrow of love
In Cupid's son

OUT OF YOUR MIND

You're outta your mind
You're outta your mind

Your soul is forgiven
Your outta your mind
Your outta your mind

Your heart has played
You for a fool
But your outta your mind
Your outta your mind

Your mettle tested
Like you run the school
Buy you outta your mind
Your outta your mind

THESE SAD SONGS

Sad songs sung for tragic hearts
With melodies and new words
And feelings so blue which hold so true
We are infected with passion calmness
And trancing
Where souls dance after a fashion
The cold weariness
These sad songs
These sad songs

Sad songs sung for broken minds
The temperate beat like a heart
Which souls play on getting nearer their goals
The timing going and coming with
Slaves of blues rhyming
The words crisp and gold the words shining
The cold weariness
These sad songs
These sad songs

Places forgotten the time gone and past
But remember those of the heart

As time of the blues comes from the start

Rhythmic pulse ignore the insults

As they come and go

And ever in the colour with mind oh so slow

The cold weariness

These sad songs

Are all we have

These sad songs

To break through pain

To face our past

These sad songs

These sad songs

Are all we have

To ease our minds

And settle broken hearts

These sad songs

These sad songs

KILLING TIMES

Time to see
Time try
Time to watch out for their lies

No need to scream and shout
Together we'll find out what it's all about
Put me in that dream around
And things will become more
On the ground

Time to see
Time to try
Time to watch out for their lies

With what we've seen going about
It's with wonder we don't all run about
Sadistic and animalistic with killing
Not willing to go on living

Time to see
Time to try
Time to watch out for their lies

It was your look that set the
Bait on the hook
It was a book that changed
My destiny
With killing times where is the
Rest of me

Time to see
Time to try
Time to watch out for their lies

GOLDEN MOON

Ooo Baby ooo baby why did you break
It in two
Like a knife cut and cracked mirror
With bad luck that leaves me so blue

Ooo baby ooo baby why couldn't you
See it through
Like a dying bird on the wing
And coldness that numbed me true

Where time with angels and hero's
The mystical beings your love your Joy
My fair re headed Maiden

The wonder of you
The bluest of black
And I give you the blues
But many lovers in the way
You know what I mean
You know what I say

Keep up never let people pull you down
Faces masks and ghost like towns

The way of the world
Laugh at the clown

Well which is which the needle pointing
The pulling of a clean stitch
But baby baby baby I'll hold onto you
For while at least
Until my wits at ease
I said baby baby baby hold onto me
Till the moon drops to its knees
And the damned scream please

Ooo angel ooo angel don't leave me to fade
Its more dangerous than night shade
Hold on angel hold on baby I'll sees you soon
On a dew dropping moon

Oooo Moon with a star that shines so true
No one cares and this I swear
It's in the air
Of a cold golden moon
Of a cold golden moon
With thieves in the shadows
And smoke in the meadows
On a dew dropping moon
Ooo baby baby baby

POEM

The night set sail and hero's began their plan
To summits of the godlike man
With quiet pen scratching at words
The food for thought was giving to the birds
And summer shower in the quiet hour
Was warmer than I thought
Even though the words were a feeling of nought
And creatures bloomed around the tomb
With wailing weeping eyes
I set myself between this worlds bitter health and
Made the monstrous disguise

SWEET LOVE

The wonder of you
The bluest of black
And I give you the blues
But many lovers in the way
You know what I mean
You know what I say

Keep hope up never let the people pull you down
Face masks and ghost like towns
The way of the world
Laugh at the clown

I wish you would come with beauty
And let me turn my hurt in loves duty
You smile whilst a tear stains this face
I wish you would come to this place
The way gone I'm wondering about certain thrills
They've gone away with yellow mellow pills
Maybe beings of light take flight
When love at first sight doesn't go right

The wonder of you

The bluest of black
And I give you the blues
But many lovers in the way
You know what I mean
You know what I say

Well dawn chasing away the night
You know my heart beats with sweet love
And iron comes warfare
With lead bullets
But I love you is not what you want
So take up the steel and forget
The sweet love
Sweet love
Sweet love
Sweet love
Sweet love

MY WORLD

The face quiet in the mirror
Quiet yet insane as any river
You bleed time with sun kisses
And warm warnings
The new throne the heart dawning
Closing doors with personality
Profound

You are my world
You are my world girl
Where do I take you angel?

Profound and round the bend
You take me away with a trend
Well some warning some hints you gave
But watching you I see nothing
The place a cold ill grave

You are my world
You are my world girl
Where do I take you baby?

The personality away batter'd
My heart and soul torn and shatter'd
The quiet word going coolly around and around
You know some people float of the ground
With time going round and round

You are my world
You are my world girl
Where do I take you angel?
SIN

Caged in hearts with sullen sunken looks
You threw me away you changed the book
My wonder of wonder
No time to steal
No time to plunder

I close my eyes to ferverant fires
Nights in honest were just desire
You became my whole heart
My wonder of wonder
No time to steal
No time to plunder

Love moving through our skies our eyes
The place heating up with desire and fire
My wonder of wonder

No time to steal
No time to plunder

The seas taking our love and tearing
It asunder with white lies like that we wonder
Begin Begin Begin
The end of sleep and a world on fire
Sin Sin Sin
The true broken promise my heart
All done
Win Win Win
Begin in sin take it all then prove
You can win

NEW SONG

There are dreams unfolding
Into the waking dawn
With holy and golden
And a new song

The silent of times new breed
Of stars which shine a new seed
And of course wondrous sounds
And a new song

My heart in worldly amusement
With whim or care
The place to be sung
The new song

Cold comes the dew on a unkept garden
Sorry for those thoughts beg your pardon
I'm quiet in those words
Of a new song

BENZIDRINE DREAM

The world we want with arising dawn
No one knows of the earth's shadows
It's set in starlight ways
Sullen puppets unknown plays
It's quiet at night
Without the comfort
Without the light
You want to hold on tight

My heart diseased wretched and poor
The golden warmth dying with rape
The scream primordial in every ear
Sullen puppets unknown seers
It's quiet at night
Without the comfort
Without the delight
You wanna hold on ooo out of sight

The morning never seems to come
Working speak and the winsome weep
With shining love that's gone away

Sullen puppets and broken laze
It's quiet at night
Without the comfort
Without you tonight
You wanna hold on for your rights

It's cold out here Dawn
It's cold out here dawn
It's cold out here Dawn
Ooo the broken morning came
Ooo the broken morning came
I'm not blaming you
I'm not blaming you I'm not blaming you
Ooo yes I do
Ooo yes I do
Ooo yes I do

POEM

With hope in the morn
I'd kiss the dawn
With night on its heels
Comfort shall steal
Away our very souls
Benzidrine dream
I've lost control
Of a delightful romance
Gone is my chance
Heartbroken with the very blues
I hope to see you oh so soon

GUNPOWDER AND AMPHETIMINE

The time to be
With moods changing
The true angel of wisdom
Will change whilst shifting

Gear all burned
Move with looks
Sure of time
Sure it's books

The faces staring
With places burning
Gunpowder amphetamine
I'll tell you what they mean to me

Gear all burned
Move with looks
Sure of time
Sure he ain't no antichrist

They mean nothing
When the world means something

Glad you are for those dreams
Even tho' they mean nothing to me

Gear all burned
Move with looks
Sure of time
Yes baby I've lost my mind

The house cold
Starvation of lust
Who do you know
And who do you trust

Gear all burned
Move with looks
Sure of time
Yes Gunpowder and amphetamine
Gunpowder and amphetamine
Gunpowder and amphetamine
You know nothing about me

TURN ME

If you were to creep in and lay next to me

The world wouldn't seem as blue I'd feel ecstasy

The heart asks questions the body wants

It's silent whilst I think of you my soul pouts

The things move the fire walks with me

I want your love I want your body next to me

I'm so lonely

I'm so lonely I'm going to nothing

If you were to love me I'd be in a world of delight

I'm hoping that day is day and night is night

The freezing winter rain saddens me takes my pride

My heart down thinking of you

Wondering whether I'm a slave

The touch so gentle with tears and sadness

Turns me

Turns me

Turns me earths grave

The things move the fire walks with me
I want your love I want your body next to me
I'm so lonely I'm so lonely I'm going to nothing

Jesus watch it's cold out there in the winters care
If you stood there quietly confused quietly bare
I'd fall so in love with this life
And the things that happen would happen

Yes I would strain your soul
I would start mapping
To worlds of beauty and worlds
That happen
Turn me
Turn me
Turn me to your love

The things move the fire walks with me
I want your love I want your body next to me
I'm so lonely I'm so lonely I'm going to nothing

The quiet way you walk
The hello you talk
My heart here just for you
To turn to any colour but blue
I want so much but you say

I love you

And that was enough to see me through

Our eyes windows to our souls

Truth it's a beautiful way to go

I wouldn't treat you bad

Wouldn't leave you sad

Wouldn't treat you like some fad

Turn me

Turn me

Turn me to your love

The things move the fire walks with me

I want your love I want your body next to me

I'm so lonely

I'm so lonely I'm going to nothing

Turn me

Turn me

Turn me

It's you

SMOKE ON IN THE BLUES

It's coming with light
The openness the night
My heart open, on the mend
The girl gone
The place smoke

Shadows with stars
People moving in the toughest bars
Never saw women with such stone
The girl gone
The place in smoke

It's quiet in this room
The girl broke my heart too soon
So smoke on in the blues
So smoke on in the blues

With time drawing in
The devil dreamed of original sin
Fire blew me your way
The girl gone
The dance to smoke

Quiet my world with angel tears
People live quiet in
This tomb of fears
The women go on their way
The girl gone
The chance to smoke

It's quiet in this room
The girl broke my heart too soon
So smoke on in the blues
So smoke on in the blues
So smoke on in the blues
So smoke on in the blues

WORLD SO CRUEL

The world of people cold
The blues all rhyming in my head
People all dancing to the dead
With a world slowly bled
Everywhere gone to a world so cruel

Take it down turn it round
To a world so cruel
The open blade the duel

Well here it comes again
Don't really care what he said
I've been through the valley of the dead
With a time of blues Spilling out my head
I've seen the holy sunlight

Take it down turn it round
To a world of bright light
The open night the fight

Well they say don't give up your day job
But this is a perfect way to express myself

And bought with gold
I'm set to hells evil soul
The people all cry but I'm going to win

With a world so cruel
Pick me up baby ooo so cool
Try life in delight
Try life in delight
Try life in delight
COMFORT SMOKE

Electric woman with looks of passion
You are truly wondrous and in fashion
The believers
The mysterious
People see us and don't know
Your world, take it real slow

You are a dream
Yes I can see you on the scene
Comfort smoke
Glad your honey
See you almost spoke

Want your eyes your soul
My heart set to your sun

But you changed your mind so suddenly
Leaving me with tears
Caution, like playing with fate

You are a dream
Yes I can see you on the scene
Comfort smoke
Glad your honey
See you almost spoke
Comfort smoke
Comfort smoke
See you almost spoke

JOKERS SMILE

The foreign mind
Whilst I lead on blind
Take it all
Take your time
My heart on the mend

Bye Bye gentle sleep
We try not to but weep
Take your time
Keep me in mind
My heart round the bend

Goodness life is everlasting
And we don't just get one
Take it all
Take your time
My soul going gradually away

Place yourself with a love
Poor and desperate dove
Take it all
Take your time
Don't change your mind

Good at last a bone

The way to go

Trace my heart

It'll calm me down

And set me away from the sound

My goings and comings

In those concrete towers

Take your time

Don't change your mind

The zoo becoming wild Jokers smile

Jokers smile

Jokers smile

Walk the mile

Jokers smile

Turning all the while

Jokers smile

Jokers laugh

Jokers laugh

Taking the tinted L.S.D bath

Bye we say to those dreams

But Jokers smile

Will show you Anarchy's L.S.D

Jokers smile

Jokers smile

Jokers laugh

Turn those cards

Turn those cards

It's the Joker

The toker

The jokers smile

Spraf up Peter

Passions Right Dream she said

Gladly I forgive

It's quiet

In the blue midnight

Yes you do

Yes you have every right

Take me down

Take me away

Lose faith in sweet delight

Lose faith in passions right

Well I've been misused I'm still caught up in drug abuse

Whilst governments light up the skies

In modern firelight

Well before you thinks another

Preaching star

I've been left with abusive scars

Take me down

Take me away

From the minister and his prayers

We turn from poison to slayers

I had answers for you about things

Which could be or couldn't be true

Love above sailing into these arms

Pink well green I run with opiate

Type dreams

And animals grow bigger in their

Open Iron farms

Take me down

Take me away

From governess the early kiss

Love is going to dissipate

The smile all the while going

The crooked mile

A close coughin bottle laced

With opium not very often you get one

If it's all burnt there must have been 30 ton

Screw this I hope they don't cotton on

Take me down

Take me away

From sisters of succubus's and dragon's slaves

LOVE IN THE NIGHT

Take a walk with me
Tell me who do you adore?
I want to tell you the truth
I want you to see the proof
About society and how it's a tomb
Get me out this room

I feel it in the air
Love in the night
Tell me babe it's got to be right

Where hells teeth mend and dark stone is right
The devil roams
Up until the final twilight
Dawn approaching fast after the score
So tell me ooo babe who do
You adore?

I feel it in the air
Love in the night
So tell me babe it's got to be right

I quietly wander these streets
At night hoping for a woman
Of dark delight
Quiet everyone the dusk is
Away and all I want to do
Is play and score
Darlin who do you adore?

Darlin who do you adore?
Darlin who do you adore?
Darlin who do you adore?
Ooo darlin don't leave me in this downpour

SHAKE A BONE

Shake a bone
Shake a bone
Shake a bone she said

Shake a bone
Shake a bone
Make her moan she said

Shake a bone
Shake a bone
Shake a bone she said

Shake a bone
Shake a bone
Make her crazy in the head

www.ingramcontent.com/pod-product-compliance
Lightning Source LLC
Chambersburg PA
CBHW031308060426
42444CB00032B/545